The Wicked West of Cromwell Street

The Wicked West of Cromwell Street

The Lives of Serial Killers Fred and Rose West

Jack Smith

Copyrights
All rights reserved. © Jack Smith and Maplewood Publishing. No part of this publication or the information in it may be quoted from or reproduced in any form by means such as printing, scanning, photocopying, or otherwise without prior written permission of the copyright holder.

Disclaimer and Terms of Use
Effort has been made to ensure that the information in this book is accurate and complete. However, the author and the publisher do not warrant the accuracy of the information, text, and graphics contained within the book due to the rapidly changing nature of science, research, known and unknown facts, and internet. The author and the publisher do not hold any responsibility for errors, omissions, or contrary interpretation of the subject matter herein. This book is presented solely for motivational and informational purposes only

ISBN-13: 978-1519492999

Printed in the United States

Warning
Throughout the book there are some descriptions of murders and crime scenes that some people might find disturbing.

MAPLEWOOD
— PUBLISHING —

Contents

Contents 5
Introduction 1
Fred West: the early years 3
Rose West: the early years 9
Their Meeting 13
Charmaine West 18
Catherine "Rena" Costello 23
Caroline Owens 27
Lynda Gough 33
Carol "Caz" Ann Cooper 38
Lucy Katherine Partington 42
Therese Siegenthaler and Shirley Hubbard 46
Juanita "Nita" Marion Mott, Shirley Anne Robinson, and Alison Chambers 50
Heather Ann West 57
The Investigation 61
The Aftermath 66
Conclusion 71
Further Reading 72
Confirmed Murders Timeline 73
Excerpt of Jack Smith's Book Serial Killers Volume 2 Exploring the Horrific True Crimes of Little Known Murderers 75
More Books from Jack Smith 89

Introduction

Modern societies are fascinated by murder. It is a constant theme throughout much of our media. Many news outlets will prioritize a murder story, knowing that it will enthrall readers. There is something about those who decide to take a life that makes them incredibly interesting to the rest of us. While many of the most famous murderers are known across the world, there are those whose crimes are relatively less known. One of the strangest stories involves the married couple of Fred and Rose West. Together, they killed. Up until the time they were caught, they engaged in a string of murders, each motivated by hate, jealousy, passion, and a fundamental lack of morals.

In this book, we will go in-depth and learn about the history of the murderers. We will examine Fred's and Rose's early lives, their relationship, their personalities, and will ultimately try and discover what it was that drove them to become two of the most notorious killers in the history of the British Isles. Though their crimes made front page news at the time, few people outside of the country know the extent of their criminality. In this book, we will learn exactly what made their killings so infamous.

For those who are in any way interested in the depths of human morality, the Wests represent some of the most depraved and sadistic murderers to have ever lived. Not only did they prey on unsuspecting young girls, but their attentions were even turned towards their own daughters. In a case involving kidnap, rape, and murder, Fred and Rose went beyond the realms of what many of us consider possible as people. Read on to learn exactly what drove Fred and Rose West to become two of history's greatest monsters.

Fred West: the early years

For our first foray into the world of Fred and Rose West, we will look into the early childhood of one of the story's main villains. Despised by many after his arrest and with others attempting to comprehend how the man they thought they knew was capable of such crimes, the life of Fred West seemed to contain little that might cause it to turn so suddenly dark. Indeed, many have looked at the surface circumstances of Fred's early years and seen little to raise an eyebrow. When we delve a little deeper, however, things take a decidedly twisted turn.

Fred West was born on 29th September, 1941. He was raised in a town named Much Marcle, in a home named Bickerton Cottage. The family lived in the county of Herefordshire, a little-known county in the west of England whose greatest claim to fame is its position as the home of the British Special Forces, the SAS. The family was poor. Fred's father, Walter West, was a laborer on a local farm. As part of the bottom rung of the village's social strata, the family was known to be poor, but Fred's parents had a reputation as being hard-working and decent people. Fred's mother, Daisy West, would go on to have eight children, though two of these died in infancy.

The house where the family lived belonged to a local farmer, Frank Brooke, who allowed his workers to live there while they were employed. It was not a big home. Until a third bedroom was added, the growing family had to divide themselves between just two rooms. Thinking back on the early days of Fred West's childhood, people have remembered him as being a normal little boy. Kay Cotton, daughter of Frank Brooke, remembers him as a cheerful lad, one who did not much stand out from a crowd. She mentions that he might have been a bit cheeky and mouthy, but remembers that as being a standard trait in boys at the time. If anything, she recollects, he might well have been naïve and easily led into trouble.

She is not alone in her recollections of the early childhood of Fred West. His aunt, Edna Hill (sister of Daisy West), remembers that the family would strive to be together a great deal of the time. They would do a lot together, including hop picking, where the whole family would venture out into the fields to help harvest the crop of hops. When talking about her sister, Edna suggests that Daisy was a fantastic mother. She says that the family, (though poor), had everything they could have wanted, and that Daisy was always accompanied by several of her children wherever she went.

It has been suggested that of all the West children, Fred was his mother's favorite. Of the three sons and three daughters, it was Fred who stood out in the ranks of his mother's affections. A schoolmate of Fred's named Ann Colburn recalls that his mother was very protective, to a greater extent than with her other children. She even remembers seeing Daisy on a number of occasions as she walked down the road towards the school, marching with intent to remonstrate with one of the teachers who had been giving her son a hard time.

School was, for Fred, a village affair. He received his education in the local school and was not a stand-out student. Once he left school, he went straight to work alongside his father on Frank Brooke's farm. This didn't hold his interest, however, and Fred departed the position after just a year and a half.

But while Fred's childhood might seem to have been a standard experience for a boy from a small village, there has since emerged a dark undercurrent. There have been numerous suggestions of abuse and incest among the various family members. Putting an exact history together of Fred's youth is tough. One of the most common claims is that his father took to sexually abusing his daughters (Fred's sisters) to the extent that it was an accepted part of the household. In addition to this, others have put forward the idea that Fred's father taught him to engage in acts of bestiality (sex with animals) from a young age, though these claims are harder to find evidence for. When being interviewed by police after his eventual capture, Fred West is on record as having said that his father always taught him that he should do exactly was he pleased, as long as he didn't get caught.

Other suggestions revolving around Fred's early life involve allegations that his mother Daisy might also have sexually abused her so-called favorite son. The stories suggest that from the age of twelve, Frank was used by Daisy in an incestuous, abusive relationship similar to the allegations levied against her husband and daughters. Despite these stories being put to Fred at a later date, they were strenuously denied. Added to this, the only surviving brother from the West family has spoken to the press on numerous occasions and denied that any abuse took place. He has labelled his brother Doug as a liar, as someone who is happy to believe in lies and fantasies, especially when regarding his life or the family's upbringing. To this extent, we may never know the truth about the abuse that may or may not have happened in the West household.

When he was seventeen years old, Fred was involved in a motorcycle accident. Crashing and being thrown from the vehicle, he was admitted to hospital with a number of serious injuries. These included not only a broken arm and leg, but also a fractured skull. Perhaps most worryingly, he was unconscious. Fred would not wake up for another week, during which time his family watched over him in the hospital. Once he regained consciousness and was able to return home, his family began to notice that he was increasingly liable to launch into fits of anger. These rage-filled incidents would be a huge change for a person normally regarded as quiet and docile. Fred would again succumb to injury when, two years later, he took a blow to the head while clambering over a fire escape. The injury left him unconscious again, though this time only for twenty-four hours.

It would be at the age of nineteen when Fred first began to experience real friction with his family. In 1960, he was placed under arrest by the local police force amid allegations that he had molested a thirteen-year-old girl. Fred was convicted of the crime but managed to escape without being sentenced to serve time behind bars. At this time, his mother refused to have him in the house. He was initially sent to live with one of his sisters on the other side of the village. Following the conviction for molestation, Fred was disowned by most of the family, who wanted little else to do with him.

Once Fred moved away from his small village upbringing, he began to become more exposed to the wider world. After quitting his position at the local farm, Fred and his brother John began to take on numerous construction jobs across west Gloucestershire. Working on numerous building sites, the pair began to grow more and more familiar with the world outside of Much Marcle. It was around this time that Fred would meet one of the most important people in his life, Catherine Costello.

Catherine was originally from Scotland but had moved to the area and taken on a position working in a café known as the Milk Bar. Located near Ledbury, it was a frequent destination for Fred and John, as well as many other young people at the time. A short while after meeting, Fred and Catherine embarked upon a romantic relationship, but Fred took the decision to keep the circumstances secret from most of his family.

Fred and Catherine got married. The only family member who had any idea that the ceremony was taking place was John. Taking on the position of the best man, John was part of the wedding, but the remaining members of the West family only discovered that Fred had gotten "hitched" at a later date. Doug West recalls that Fred simply arrived home one day and informed the family that he had become a married man. At first, the family thought the whole thing was a joke.

The decision to keep the relationship and the marriage secret was – for Doug – indicative of Fred as a person. At those times when he knew he wanted something, he just went ahead and did it. All the while, there was an air of secrecy about the man, with Fred unwilling to divulge all of the information at any one time. From the outside, he appeared as an easy-going man, a straightforward kind of person who few suspected possessed a hidden dark side.

The marriage to Catherine would prove to be a major factor in Fred's life when he met another woman named Rose. Before we get started on that story, however, we should learn more about the woman who would eventually become Rose West. For Fred's parents, Walter and Daisy, they never lived to see the monster that their son would become. They passed away and are still buried in Much Marcle. When thinking back on the couple, Kay Cotton recalls Walter as a "nice old boy," a man who would have found Fred's crimes to be horrifying.

Despite the suggestions and legends of abuse committed in the household, few could have expected the young Fred West to grow up into the man he would eventually become.

Rose West: the early years

These days, Rose West has a reputation that has perhaps exceeded that of her husband. Her involvement in the series of murders is notorious, possibly due to the much smaller number of female serial killers which we are likely to encounter. Despite the large number of recognized serial killers the world has seen, few have actually been women. In this respect, Rose West is something of a rarity. Because of this, interest in her life is especially strong. Just like with Fred, if we are to understand her motivations for killing so many people, we should first look at her upbringing and the time before she met Fred. Here, we find an even stranger story than the one belonging to the man she eventually married. It all starts before she was even born.

Rosemary West was born in 1953 in Devon, twelve years after Fred. Her birthday was the 29th of November, but before she had even arrived in this world, she had been subjected to strange medical treatments. Her mother, coincidently also named Daisy, had suffered from a long-standing problem with depression. This became especially prevalent during her pregnancy. It was only then that her doctors resolved to do something about the matter. At the time, many mental health issues were still very much misunderstood, and treatments for conditions such as depression were raw and unrefined, at best. At worst, they were almost brutal. Unfortunately for Daisy and her unborn child, her doctors decided to veer towards one of the more brutal methods.

While still pregnant with baby Rose, Daisy was treated with electroconvulsive therapy. No longer used by modern medical practitioners, the procedure involves passing electric currents through the brain of the patient. In turn, this triggers a seizure and causes changes in the brain's chemical make-up. It was thought that this process would be able to reverse the symptoms of some patients' suffering from mental health conditions. According to some studies, the modern version of the procedure (if absolutely essential) can be deemed to pose few risks to pregnant women, should the correct steps be taken. However, the equivalent procedure during the 1950s in Britain likely failed to take such matters into account. For some researchers and biographers, the electroconvulsive therapy endured by Daisy at this time played a large role in the development of Rose as a child.

After being born, Rose was not raised in a happy household. Her parents' marriage has been described as turbulent and it was not uncommon for violence to be present in the home. Her father was prone to lashing out at her mother, eventually leading Daisy to leave and take Rose with her. Throughout her childhood, Rose struggled with a number of mental health concerns. Her occasional weight problems caused much consternation, while her poor performances in her school were a constant source of disappointment. Much like her father, occasional bouts of aggressive behavior were not uncommon. As various biographers have noted, her sexual and romantic interests throughout her teenage years and beyond seemed to demonstrate a particular interest in older men. She was known to be sexually active.

Rose was one of seven children. Despite being born in Devon, the family would later move to Cheltenham in Gloucester. After her mother and father argued and split, she went to live with her aunt. With all seven children and Daisy, the family moved into the home of Glenys in Cheltenham. Rose got a job and began working in the local area, but her mother was not able to settle. One day, on returning home from work, Rose found that her mother and her brothers had gone. Confused, she asked a sister what had happened and where they had vanished to. Her sister replied that they had simply moved on. Abandoned by her mother and half her family, Rose would eventually reveal to a courtroom that the event has a "devastating effect" on her.

During this time, she was the victim of two rapes. The first came before the departure of her mother, when Rose was aged just fifteen years old. Following a Christmas party, Rose was walking home. A stranger in a car pulled over and offered her a lift. Reluctantly, Rose acquiesced. The unnamed man then drove her past her home, continuing to drive further away and out into the nearby hills. Here, he raped Rose, who recalled that she thought her life to be in danger and assumed that the man was going to kill her. She never told her parents. At the time that her mother was thinking of leaving the family yet again, Rose was raped again. This time, the attack took place at a bus stop. A man approached her while she waited for the next bus. He began to talk to the young girl and frightened Rose enough that she tried to run away. The man caught up to her and dragged her out of sight and into a parking lot before raping her.

At this time, Rose decided to move back into her father's home. She was sixteen. As well as this, she took the decision to start using a different bus, one that was far removed from the bus stop where she had been attacked. This new bus journeyed through Cheltenham's main bus shelter, and it was here that she first encountered a man named Fred West. Her life at home was still far from perfect. Despite moving back into her father's house, she was again suffering at his hands. Allegedly a paranoid schizophrenic, Rose's father began to exhibit his violent tenancies again. Rather than hitting his wife, he began to strike his daughter. There have even been suggestions that he sexually abused his teenage daughter, though these have not been verified. Despite this violence (or perhaps because of it) Rose kept her first romantic forays with Fred West far from her father's attention.

After Rose met Fred, neither of their lives would ever be the same again. Even after suffering from a horrific early childhood, Rose gradually began to notice that she could trust Fred. In him, she encountered a man who shared many of her worst experiences and who could exhibit real empathy toward her. Together, they would eventually form a terrible bond. However, when they first met, Fred was already married to another woman. In the next chapter, we will discover exactly how Fred and Rose West took the first steps towards becoming the infamous couple we know today.

Their Meeting

While both Fred and Rose West had difficult childhoods, it was only after they met that they would begin to reveal the extreme evil of which they were capable. Before they could properly get together, however, there was a problem. Catherine Costello.

During September of 1962, Fred West had become reacquainted with Catherine and would eventual marry her. Fred and Catherine had been in a relationship, but it had fallen apart. This love interest was rekindled and soon the two were inseparable. Catherine was not the sweet and innocent girl she might have appeared, however. Instead, she had first gotten to know Fred through a working relationship. Catherine was more commonly known by the name Rena. Working as a prostitute, she was already pregnant by the time she and Fred got married. Together, they decided to move to Coatbridge in the county of Lanarkshire.

A daughter was born to the couple in 1963, on the 22nd of February. The actual father had been a client of Catherine, a Pakistani bus driver whose name she would not reveal. Due to the race of the father, the baby's appearance might have caused difficulty for the couple. Instead, they informed friends that they had adopted the child, who they named Charmaine Carol West. A year later, the couple would have a daughter of their own, Anne Marie, who was born in July of 1964.

During this time, Fred West was working as an ice cream man. His simple job would amount to driving around the various housing estates and selling ice cream to the enthusiastic children. The van played music as he drove around and, occasionally, a crowd would follow behind him on hot days, eager to purchase ice cream treats. But the job was not as pure and innocent as might have been. In fact, on the 4th of November, 1965, Fred was involved in an incident in which a young boy was killed. While he was driving the ice cream van, Fred hit a four-year-old. The little boy died. Though he did not face murder charges for the death, Fred feared that he might face retaliation from the community.

Together, Fred, Catherine, their two children, and the children's nanny decided to move home. They packed their bags and made their way to Gloucestershire, where a young Rose was already living. Following the tragedy of the little boy hit by the ice cream van, Fred was increasingly wary of the chances that he might face repercussions for his actions. Though this limited his public life, it did not stop the violent outbursts at home. Together, the family and Isa McNeill, who briefly became their nanny – along with another woman named Anne McFall – moved into a caravan park in Bishop's Cleeve.

At this time, the loving relationship between Catherine and Fred had evaporated. Along with the violent outbursts that had become a frequent occurrence in Fred's life, he was beginning to make increasingly sadistic sexual demands. His requests and order reached a breaking point in 1966, when Catherine decided that she would have to leave Fred. Along with Isa McNeill, she left the children behind and fled to Scotland. Both the young girls, Charmaine and Anne, stayed behind with their father, as well as Anne McFall, who volunteered to help with the child care. In actual fact, she had become infatuated with Fred West. Their relationship eventually became sexual, and McFall became pregnant with Fred's child. Though Catherine returned every few months to visit her children, it was Anne who became the key female figure in Fred's life, despite his legal marriage to his actual wife.

This ceased to be an issue in August of 1967. At the time, Anne McFall was eight months pregnant, when she simply vanished. During the time of her disappearance, not a single person reported her as missing. There were no complaints or concerns filed with the police. It would be another thirty years before investigators were able to solve the case, when Anne McFall's body was found in a local field. It had been buried there after she had been killed. Along with the boy killed by Fred's ice cream truck, she is thought to be one of the earliest victims of Fred's homicidal rage, along with the child she was carrying inside her.

Following the disappearance of Anne McFall, Catherine spent time flitting back and forth between Scotland and the caravan park. For one extended period, she actually returned to the home and took care of the children. She could never bear to be in Fred's company for too long, however, and it did not take much time before she once again left him. Again, the children were left with their father, who was now forced to look after them on his own. It was in this context that Fred would fall in love with Rose. Married to an estranged wife, raising two daughters (one of which was not his own), in a caravan park, after potentially murdering two people, Fred West was far from many people's idea of an ideal prospective husband. For Rose, it did not matter.

As mentioned in the previous chapter, Fred West met Rosemary Letts when she had to change her bus route. Still living with her father at this point, she was twelve years Fred's junior. When they first met, Rose was still only fifteen years old. In fact, they first met on the day she turned fifteen. A year later, the day she turned sixteen, she moved into Fred's house. Despite the whirlwind nature of their romance, Rose recalls that her first impressions of Fred were ones of horror. It was only after he spent a huge amount of time persistently asking her out on a date that she agreed to go out with him. The two went to a village pub.

While they were courting, the relationship was kept hidden from Rose's father. Correctly assuming that he would disapprove of the bond the two were forming, they tried to keep it a secret for as long as possible. When he did uncover the truth, he threatened to report Fred to Social Services. Speaking about the relationship when she was eventually put on trial, Rose told the courts how Fred has "promised her the world." Due to her young age, she recollected that she was not aware of the nature of his lies and truly believed Fred. Rose remembered that he promised to love her and care for her, claims that she later said were lies.

After the pair moved in together, Rose was sharing her new home with Fred's daughters, Charmaine and Anne. Moving out of the caravan, the unconventional family moved to a new address on Midland Road. The home was larger than the caravan and was intended to make room for the growing family.

Rose and Fred West would eventually get married in 1972. The family reached a decision to move into the bigger house, after which we begin to see the seeds sown for the future crimes committed by the couple.

Fred, likely already a murderer by this point, had married a girl twelve years younger than himself, in defiance of her father, and had been demonstrating signs of an explosive temperament. Rose, scarred by her tumultuous upbringing, had turned towards the one man who had consistently shown her affection. Together, the two would prod, probe, and push one another to terrible, new heights. And in the middle of it all, Fred's two daughters were living in the same home. In the next chapter, we will discover what happened to one of the children and how this influenced the lives of many others.

Charmaine West

Charmaine West was related to neither Fred nor Rose West. As mentioned previously, she was the adopted daughter of Fred, a product of his first marriage to Catherine Costello. Not only this, but she was born to Catherine as the result of her activity as a prostitute. Her father was bus driver who had been one of her mother's clients. But she was not the only child to be raised in the house.

As well as Charmaine, Fred's legitimate daughter from his first marriage, Anne, lived with the newlyweds. It was into this non-traditional set up that Rose brought the couple's first baby of their own. Born in October of 1970, the child was named Heather Anne. Just two months after her birth, Fred was arrested and thrown in jail. He had been convicted of theft and was set to serve a six-month sentence. During this time, Rose was left alone at home with Charmaine, Anne, and Heather.

The home was not a happy one. With her husband taken away from her, Rose was beginning to feel lonely. With three young girls, only one of which was her daughter, she struggled to take care of all of the children. As well as the effort of the childcare itself, Rose's temper did not help. She was known to exhibit signs of resentment towards the children from Fred's previous marriage and showed a clear bias towards her own daughter in terms of the love and attention she lavished upon the children.

Charmaine was old enough to attend school, but her record of showing up was not always perfect. With little motivation from Rose to see her attend school regularly, coupled with the changes in address that the family was undertaking, the authorities failed to notice that Charmaine was not in attendance in the correct and proper fashion. With Fred not around to supply his own support for the children and with Rose left to her own devices, both Anne and Charmaine began to receive less-than-perfect care.

It is thought that Rose West killed Charmaine West in June of 1971, just before Fred was released from jail. At the time,

Rose's treatment of the two girls from the previous marriage was reaching a demonic level. Frequently she would verbally and physically abuse the children. Both Anne and Charmaine were subject to severe beatings on a regular basis. While Anne broke down in tears on many occasions, Charmaine only angered Rose further by refusing to show any signs of pain. Regardless of how much she was punished by her adoptive mother, she refused to cry. In mid-June, it seemed as though this finally caused Rose to snap. Charmaine disappeared.

There were few people around to notice the vanishing of a young girl. With Fred still serving his jail sentence, Catherine Costello still in Scotland, and Anne West under the threat of further beatings from Rose should she dare mention anything to anyone, there was no one who might notice the disappearance of the little girl. For anyone who did ask – typically in a conversational fashion – Rose explained the situation by claiming that Charmaine's mother had arrived and taken her back to Scotland. No one thought to check up on this story, and it was held as gospel truth among the community.

Fred West arrived home from prison to find that Rose had murdered his adopted daughter. Rather than go to the authorities, he chose to involve himself in the crime and sought to cover up his wife's actions. First, he severed the fingers and toes from the little girl's body. He tore up the floor of the kitchen in the house and buried the mutilated corpse of his adoptive daughter underneath. Covering her back up, he re-laid the floor and covered up any traces that something might be hidden beneath.

At the time of her death, Charmaine was just eight years old. Her killer was just seventeen. When examining the evidence at the trial of Rose West, Brian Leveson told the court of the huge amount of evidence that demonstrated beyond a doubt that Charmaine was intensely disliked by Rose. In particular, the adoptive teenage mother found the child's rebellious nature to be absolutely loathsome. Of the evidence that was gathered during the case, one report came from a girl known as Charmaine's best friend. When calling on the home to borrow a small amount of milk, the girl walked into the West's house to find Charmaine standing on a chair in the middle of the kitchen. Her hands had been tied behind her back using a leather belt. Next to her, Rose stood with a large wooden spoon in her hand. The little girl had told her mother, who had in turn asked Rose about the event. Rose had simply dismissed it as a punishment for bad behavior. Unfortunately, it was likely just one incident in a string of abusive behaviors inflicted before Charmaine was finally killed. When described, the lie that Charmaine had gone to live with her real mother, Anne West recounted being told by Rose that the girl's departure was a "good riddance."

Following Fred West's arrival back at the home and his burial of Charmaine beneath the kitchen floor, the family life grew no less turbulent. It was around this time that the couple finally got married. Just a year after the death of Charmaine West, Rose gave birth to her second daughter, whom they called Mae. She would be the second of seven children that Rose would eventually give birth to in the relationship.

Charmaine West might not have been the first person who either Fred or Rose West killed, but it was the first time that both were complicit in the murder. Though Rose was eventually convicted of the killing, the disposal of the body bore all of the hallmarks that would eventually become associated with Fred. The removal of the fingers and toes, as well as the burying of the body on the property, would eventually become frequent occurrences as the couple began to kill again and again. Though only a child, Charmaine's life was filled with sadness and tragedy. Her death would directly lead into the demise of the next person to fall victim to Fred and Rose West.

Catherine "Rena" Costello

The death of Charmaine West, while a tragedy, proved to be a problem to the West couple for a different reason. Only a month after the disappearance of the eight-year-old girl, her mother came to collect her. Catherine Costello, Fred's former wife, had been living in Scotland and making frequent trips back to Gloucester to check in on the daughters of her previous marriage. Her impetuous nature and her choice of an alternative lifestyle as well as her frequent trips between the west of England and Scotland meant that she was a hard woman to keep track off. This would eventually prove to work in the Wests' favor.

Before fatefully becoming embroiled in the life of Fred West, Catherine's life was already less than the ideal she had once dreamed of living. Her choice of career might have turned her into a cold and cynical woman, but friends and family who knew her from Scotland remember her as something else entirely. One neighbor from her time in Glasgow remembered her as a "nice young woman" and mentioned that, despite Costello's young age, she was "exceptionally nice" and a good neighbor. On the occasions when she would bring her two little girls to live with her in Glasgow, onlookers recall that the children were always immaculate.

Despite her profession, those who remember her seem to have had been given no hint towards her wild lifestyle. A lady named May Jackson, who lived in Scotland near Catherine, remembers her only as a good mother, whose children loved her so deeply that they clung to her leg at all times.

As well as her career selling her body, Catherine also spent time working as a conductor on a bus. This was where she met Charmaine's father, as well as becoming involved with a man named John McLachlan. The two embarked upon a romantic relationship, during which time Fred West was still working as an ice cream man. The relationship did not end happily, and McLachlan, a bus driver, remembers having to go to his superiors to request that he not be put on the same bus as his lover so as to avoid her on-going pursuit of him.

By the time Catherine has become deeply wrapped up in the life of Fred West, John McLachlan remembers the last time he spoke to her. One day, out of the blue, he received a phone call from Catherine Costello. During the conversation, she begged John for help. Fred, she confided in him, was once again turning violent. Scared for her life and the lives of her daughters, she asked that John do something to help her. He should arrive in secret, she suggested, and help her flee. However, the plan was uncovered by Anne McFall, and Fred found out. This proved to be the final straw. Catherine fled back to Scotland to try and escape her abusive husband. She was unable to take the children with her.

Isolated and kept away from the children for extended periods, Catherine was only able to see Charmaine and Anne when permitted. This meant that the long journey down from Scotland was not as regular as she might have liked it to be. One day, on arriving back at the house Fred was now sharing with Rose, Catherine discovered that her oldest daughter was nowhere to be found. Charmaine, actually buried under the kitchen floor, was seemingly not in the house. This angered Catherine, who demanded to see her daughter.

We know very little of the actual murder. Catherine "Rena" Costello vanished during August just as her daughter had. What we do know is that later investigations found the body. Just like with Charmaine, the fingers and the toes had been cut away from the body before burial. This was what led investigators to believe that it had likely been the work of Fred West.

Once Catherine Costello had been killed, there was little that stood in the way of Rose and Fred's murderous relationship. Together, they had killed the adopted daughter and the meddling (at least, as they saw her) ex-wife. Unlike Catherine, Rose seemed to be the ideal woman for Fred. In her, he found a woman who was utterly infatuated with him. While he had chosen Catherine for her sexual proclivity, in Rose he found a young girl who was willing to do exactly as he requested.

After murdering both his daughter and ex-wife and with another baby soon to arrive, the couple decided that they would need to move into a bigger house. Not only were they willing to leave behind the bodies they had buried at the property, but they needed more space. The space was not only for the soon-to-arrive Mae West, but also for the big plans that Fred had lying ahead. As such, they made the move to a property at 25 Cromwell Road. In due course, this would come to be one of the most famous houses in Britain.

The house was not quite fit for purpose. Over the course of time, Fred himself would begin to make various adjustments. Among these alterations was the fact that Fred encouraged Rose to take in lodgers. This would provide for a source of extra income, but would also allow for Fred to welcome new people into the house, essential for his plans over the coming years. As well as a small bar and rooms designed for the children, one of the most important rooms in the house at 25 Cromwell Street would be what was known as "Rose's Room." After talking to his wife, Fred convinced Rose to start selling herself as a prostitute.

With a growing family and a growing interest in matters of a sexual nature, the events that took place over the coming years could be considered extreme even for a couple who had already killed a number of people.

Caroline Owens

One of the key figures in this story is one of the only women who came under the direct control of Fred and Rose West and managed to live to tell the tale. During the autumn of 1972, it became clear that the growing family and Rose's burgeoning career as a prostitute seemed incompatible. Purely from a scheduling standpoint, Fred's encouragement of Rose towards his choice of career meant she had little time to care for the children. Because of this, they decided that they needed some help.

Rose gradually began to engage in sexual intercourse with the other men who began to live in the house. Rose later told a jury about how Fred would take them to "Rose's Room" for sexual intercourse with. In doing so, he seemed to exist in an awkward psychological state. Despite wanting his wife to have sex with these men, Fred would then appear to be jealous of them. One of the changes he made to the house was to install a peep hole in the room to allow him to watch as Rose entertained her clients and the lodgers. Another was a red light installed outside "Rose's Room." When this was on, it was a sign for the children that they were not to enter. It meant that their mother was busy.

One of the regular clients who came to visit Rose in a professional capacity was her father. Fred encouraged the incestuous relationship. Bill Letts would pay frequent visits and pay to have sex with his daughter. With both Fred and Rose coming from abusive, possibly incestuous backgrounds, their actions as adults have frequently been tied back to their upbringing by psychological investigators.

Once the clients left and Fred started talking to his wife, he would use what Rose described as "emotional blackmail." Using her infidelity as a metaphorical stick with which to beat her, he would demonstrate extreme jealousy of the men who had come into this home and had sex with his wife, despite the fact that it was his idea. As well as his psychological abuse, Fred was not afraid to lash out with his fists and domestic violence was not uncommon in the house.

This was the situation into which Fred and Rose decided that they would need to bring a nanny to take care of the children. Rather than taking an ad out in the local paper or searching for a childcare professional, Fred decided to attempt to replicate his emotional manipulation once again. One night when driving with Rose on an isolated country road, they came across a runaway teenager. This was Caroline Owens. They picked the young girl up and listened to her story, which told of her escape from a cruel and abusive stepfather. It took just a week for her to move into 25 Cromwell Street and to take on a position as the couple's nanny.

Rather than explain to Caroline that she was working as a prostitute, Rose explained to the girl that she was a masseuse. This seemed to be a suitable explanation for the string of men who would visit on a daily basis. Living in the household, Caroline soon began to notice the strange behaviors and actions of her hosts. When talking to Fred on one occasion, she was informed that he was able to provide abortions for her, should she ever require one while in his employ. While she was staying in the house, he informed her, he was well-equipped to perform these medical procedures whenever she wanted. This raised her suspicions, especially when Fred later boasted of all of the abortions he had previously provided to numerous women, and how they would in turn reward him with sexual favors. After a few weeks in the house, she was invited into what Fred and Rose described as their "sex circle." She declined and left the house after a few weeks.

On December the 6th, 1972, Fred and Rose went out looking for Caroline. They found her again, walking down the same country road. As Rose later told a court room, Fred had encouraged her to enter into a homosexual relationship with Caroline, an experience that would have been the first lesbian encounter for Rose. In order for Rose to act out Fred's wishes, they would need to bring the young girl back.

Meeting up once again with Caroline on that isolated country road, the couple began to apologize repeatedly for their actions. They said they were sorry for what they had done to Caroline and that they wished to make it up to her. In order to do so, they invited her around to the house for a cup of tea. Caroline believed them to be sincere. It was her belief that, rather than attempting to manipulate her, the couple had simply misunderstood the job description. She hoped to accept their apology and hopped in the car to join them for that fateful cup of tea. Together, they drove back to 25 Cromwell Street. They poured her a cup of hot tea, before Rose began to take matters further. Talking at a later time, Rose remembered that she had wanted to stop as soon as she felt some resistance from Caroline. However, Fred encouraged her to do otherwise. When trying to describe what happened next, she said that she did not remember it at all.

However, Caroline's memory remains intact. According to her later description of events, Rose began to kiss her repeatedly. Despite her resistance, the couple overpowered the teenager. They bound her by the hands and feet, tying her limbs together with bondage tape. Once she was tied up, both Fred and Rose began to rape her. Her memories from the event remain surprisingly intact. She can recall that Fred, at one point, remarked that he felt her vagina to be unusual and that he resolved to change it to better suit his preferences. Whenever she would try to scream out, whether calling for help or expressing her pain, Rose would smother her face with a pillow. To try and put a stop to her struggling, the couple bound her around the neck as well.

Fred began to threaten the girl. Leaning into her ear, he promised that he would let a number of "black men" who were Rose's clients use Caroline for whatever purposes they wanted. Fred said that as soon as they were done, he would kill her and bury the body beneath the paving stones that lined the streets of Gloucester. In turn, he boasted of all the women he had killed over the years, a figure that seemed to stretch into the hundreds. The police, he suggested, would never be able to catch him.

Caroline was scared for her life. The only way she saw to possibly survive was to allow the Wests to have their way with her and hope for a chance of escape in the future. She stopped putting up a fight. Despite his promises to lock her up in the cellar, the next day Fred made Caroline promise that she would resume her position as the family nanny. Once she had promised, Fred allowed her to leave the house. Caroline went straight to the police. She told them exactly what had happened.

The police acted, and Fred and Rose were arrested. However, before the trial could reach the courts, Caroline withdrew her accusation of rape. As such, the case fell apart. Fred and Rose West pleaded guilty to the reduced charges of indecent assault. Rather than jail time, they faced a £50 fine.

When she later looked back on the events at her trial, Rose commented that she was scared throughout the entire rape of Caroline Owens. In her words, she was "as much a victim" as Caroline. Choosing to blame the incident on her husband's emotional manipulation and abuse, she tried to extricate herself from the crime.

However, future victims of Fred and Rose West would fall prey to the skills the couple had learned that night. Rather than letting future victims go, they discovered that Fred was not able to control every woman to the level he believed he could. Had the couple been fully convicted of the rape of Caroline Owens, it seems likely that they would have been unable to carry out the future murders. We can only speculate as to why Caroline dropped the charges. Whether she was intimidated, sympathetic, or genuinely believed the Wests to be innocent, we just don't know.

Regardless, the fine allowed both Fred and Rose to return to 25 Cromwell Street. Over the course of the next few years, their work would take on a more secretive edge. The account of Caroline Owens gives us an insight into how the couple treated their victims, especially useful as so many perished. Up until the full extent of their crimes was revealed to the investigators and the general public, this was perhaps the closest the Wests came to being caught during the murder spree they later embarked upon. In the next chapters, we will see their morality take on a more homicidal turn as they begin to commit the murders that made them so notorious.

Lynda Gough

After their encounter with Caroline Owens, the Wests took extra measures to ensure they were never in danger of being caught. At the same time, their capacity to commit evil deeds began to increase. One of the victims was none other than their daughter, Anne-Marie. By now eight years old, she was the same age as Charmaine had been when she had been murdered by Rose. By the time early 1973 rolled around, Fred had already introduced incest into the household. While Rose was busy entertaining her clients, Fred was focused on the daughters who were already in his home. As well as watching Rose while she had sex with numerous men, he would take Anne down into the cellar and rape her. The roles were reversed. While Anne-Marie was bound and gagged, Fred would proceed to overpower and molest her while Rose would watch on. This happened repeatedly.

The cellar under Cromwell Street became one of the most dangerous places in Britain. This was the spot where Fred and Rose would lure young girls and where they took their own daughters to molest and rape. When renovating the house, one neighbor remembers Fred joking around, mentioning that he would use his construction skills to build a torture dungeon, soundproofing the walls to make sure he was never caught. The neighbor took it as a joke, but it was not far removed from the truth. In actual fact, the entire house was being altered and changed in order to better accommodate Fred and Rose's evil desires.

While we have little evidence of what actually took place inside the cellar (due to the fact that so few victims lived to tell the tale), we can put together an accurate idea of what was likely to have taken place. For example, we know that it was typical for Fred to bind and gag his victims. They would be hung up using ropes, stripped of their clothes, and left for extended periods of time. During these periods, the West couple would inflict extreme amounts of pain and torture upon their victims. Occasionally, they might pause to have sex with one another, titillated by the horrific acts they were performing on the young girls under their control.

One of the defining aspects of Fred's character at this time was his lack of restraint. Never one to hold back on his urges, he was becoming increasingly volatile and likely to simply act out on his terrible desires. As his father had told him many years ago, he was free to do whatever he wanted, so long as he did not get caught. This lack of restraint manifested itself as a constant desire to see others in pain. Deriving a sexual pleasure from the suffering of others, Fred West seemed immune from the distaste or empathy most people might experience when witnessing another person suffering. Dr. David Holmes reviewed the case and came to the conclusion that West never experienced the "same sense of revulsion" for pain in others, especially when stripping a body or figuring out exactly how he would dispose of it. Holmes suggests that the industrious and considered approach West took to these practices engendered him with an energy that was different from many other serial killers.

Another of Fred West's innovations around the home involved him fitting a beam across the ceiling of the cellar. Into the beam, he screwed a number of hooks. There were used to hang the bound victims, sometimes for several days. Once the girls had been murdered, their corpses would remain hanging from the hooks and be allowed to mummify. Eventually, the bodies would be taken apart by an eager and diligent Fred, before he buried the remains underneath the floor of the cellar. Rose, too, became practiced in the art of dismembering a corpse. It was not uncommon for the two to share the responsibilities of taking apart their victims.

One professor who looked over the case after the conviction, Professor Bernard Knight, noted the removal of the heads from the bodies, added to the small cuts shown along the vertebrae of the victims. Legs were removed from the body at the hip and there was frequently small cut marks notched around the head of the bones in the thigh. In Knight's opinion, the job was handled with skill. Eventually, the number of bodies under the floor would become so high as to become an issue. To deal with this, Fred West simply concreted over the floor and turned the room into a playroom for the children, complete with pictures of clowns and cowboys on the wall.

As they perfected their approach to murder, the number of victims began to rack up. Among the first to die was a woman named Lynda Gough. She came into the Wests' life in 1973 and was initially just a lodger at 25 Cromwell Street. While many of the other victims were simply preyed upon and picked up by the couple, Lynda was welcomed into the home and spent time living in the house before she met her untimely end.

Gradually, Lynda was introduced to the West's alternative lifestyle. As they eased her into their way of life, Fred began to use his manipulative skills to try and convince her to become part of their "sex circle." Unlike with Caroline, this time it worked. Within a short space of time, she was sharing sexual partners with Rose. As well as Fred, who would watch the two women engaging in sexual activities, she began to sleep with the women who came to call on Rose in her capacity as a prostitute. Once she fell into the West's devious games, she was fatally trapped.

We know little of her eventual demise, other than the fact that she went missing sometime in April of 1973. Based on the information we have gathered from the other cases, as well as the details of Fred's growing dungeon in the basement, it was likely that her death was not a peaceful affair. While she may have initially engaged in sexual activity with the couple of her own free will, it is likely that she was both raped and tortured before being killed. Regardless of the exact details, she was never seen again, until her remains were found when the cellar floor was excavated.

To add an extra tragic element to the story, Lynda's death did not go entirely unnoticed. Knowing of her then-current address, Lynda's mother called on the Wests' house in order to try and find her daughter. After having not heard from her in some time, she was incredibly concerned. Rose opened the door. The first thing Mrs. Gough noticed was the fact that Rose appeared to be wearing some of Lynda's clothes and her slippers. When she asked about the whereabouts of her daughter, Rose West informed the woman that Lynda had travelled to Weston-super-Mare in order to search for employment. Despite the obvious concern on the part of Lynda's mother, no investigation by the police took place. She was simply added to the list of missing women.

While she was one of the first, Lynda Gough was by no means the only victim. Her death provided the template, and the process of her murder would become more familiar as the West couple became more incidental with their destructive, horrific behaviors. As well as incestuous rape, the house would soon come to see the arrival of any young woman as something of a death sentence.

Carol "Caz" Ann Cooper

One of the most terrifying aspects of the murder spree undertaken by Fred and Rose West was the age of their victims. Their typical approach was to prey on the weak and the defenseless. Just like with the abduction of Caroline Owens, they often chose to focus their efforts on capturing teenage girls. These victims were often from abusive backgrounds and running away from home. They were vulnerable and in difficult situations. With their experience coming from similar backgrounds and added to their sadistic inclinations, both Fred and Rose found these girls easy to manipulate and easy to persuade to step into their home. Once these girls crossed over the threshold of 25 Cromwell Street, they were often never seen again.

It helped that the two had clearly defined roles within the murders. While both would enjoy the act, Fred and Rose each had their respective responsibilities during every killing. For Rose, abuse was the key characteristic. She remained in control of the situation, keeping an eye on everything and ensuring that the girls were sufficiently under control. Fred's role was markedly different. While Rose sought to keep control, he allowed himself to succumb to every emotional impulse. In doing so, he would push through any apparent boundaries in the realms of sadism and bondage. Combined, they seemed to be a terrifying duo, utterly able to control, abuse, manipulate, and ultimately kill their teenage victims.

But their indulgence was not fixed. Rather than following an exact template, the sadistic nature of the killings only drove each of the partners on to horrible new heights. After becoming familiar with just what they had to do in order to elicit a scream from any of their victims, they would know for next time what was required and would be able to do it at will. This was torture as an inquisitive type of play, with each partner pushing the other to see just what they could do to exact an ever-increasing kind of torment on the poor victims. As their knowledge of torture and its effects on the human body increased, they were able to cause more and more pain. They could control the situation, keeping victims alive for longer and longer, in increasing states of perpetual pain. As the victims were bound and gagged, they could do little to prevent Fred or Rose West from carrying out any merciless impulse which crossed either of their minds.

Spotting the right victims was just another art that they spent their time perfecting. Following their near arrest and conviction with Caroline Owens, additional care was taken in cultivating the right kind of girls for their indulgences. Perhaps more importantly, the girls who were chosen were far less likely to be let out of the home ever again. However, just as they picked up Caroline on the side of an empty country lane, they continued to use their method to track down potential victims. There was a special class of girl whom the couple wanted to prey on, those who they referred to as "less than dead." This phrase came to mean those who could be taken into the West's home, raped, and then killed without people causing a fuss. Rather than having girls' mothers turning up on their doorstep once again, they wanted to be sure that their victims would not be missed. This meant taking the decision to focus on prostitutes, girls who had run away from home, and those who had become estranged enough from any friends and family that their vanishing would not cause consternation.

Often, the girls would be found during an evening drive. It was not uncommon for Fred and Rose to venture out in their car and drive through the parts of Gloucester where their specific type of victim might be found. This meant the areas where the sex-workers frequented, the areas where young girls might run away to, as well as the sides of roads where they might be trying to hitchhike and get a lift out of the area. Finding girls in these positions often meant that they were likely to fit the pattern and be a prime target for the murderous intentions of the couple.

One of the girls who they picked up was Carol Cooper. Known as "Caz" to her friends, Carol was fifteen at the time she had her run-in with the Wests. They came across her as they might come across many girls, as Carol walked home alone from a cinema. She was a lonely girl, living in a children's home in the nearby town of Worchester. Fitting the profile almost perfectly, Fred and Rose picked her up in their car and proceeded to take her to 25 Cromwell Street.

Without a family to come looking, the type of girl who might be in a children's home during the early 1970s might also have been the type of child who the Wests would assume would not be missed. Considering that girls of "her type" liable to run away at the drop of a hat, they assumed that those who were working in the children's home would not be as active in their pursuit of the missing girl as a parent might be. Because of this, she seemed to be the perfect next victim. She was led into the cellar to meet her demise.

We don't know when exactly Carol died. Based on the autopsy report of the mangled corpse that was recovered from beneath the basement floor, estimates put her death as having occurred sometime in November of 1973. Though she was eventually reported missing, we only know that she was picked up after her visit to the cinema. How long she was kept alive in the cellar and subjected to all manners of torture, we can only guess. For many of the girls, it was not uncommon to be kept alive for days as Fred and Rose acted out their every depraved fantasy.

Though we know little of Carol Cooper, her death served to illustrate the more refined approach to murder that the Wests were taking. With her demographic and position within society allowing them to take full advantage of her misery, her death would pave the way for similar fates in many other girls.

Lucy Katherine Partington

One of the victims for whom we know more information is Lucy Katherine Partington. Born in 1952 on the 4th of March, her death can show us a great deal about the process by which the victims were often selected, seduced, and sadistically killed by Fred and Rose West. Despite this, we still do not know much about the actual abduction itself. Unlike many of the other victims, Lucy was slightly older than a teenager. Twenty-two at the time of her death, it is suspected that she was able to put up more of a fight than the other girls. Unlike with many victims, her extra age could have made her better able to fight back against the couple, as well as keeping her more aware of their potential for violence. Despite this, she ultimately faced the same fate as those who stepped down into the cellar of 25 Cromwell Street.

Lucy Partington was not a prostitute or involved in the sex industry. She was not from an abusive background and not trying to run away from anything. While the majority of the victims all seemed to fit one template, her abduction acts as something of an outlier. It can be read as demonstrable that despite Fred and Rose's increased caution when selecting victims, they still remained creatures of instinct. Once they had identified Lucy as a potential target, any thought that she might not have seemed suitable did not enter their minds.

In late 1974, the house on Cromwell Street was becoming more and more a home for depraved acts. Not only had Fred worked hard to attune it to his exact needs, but he had worked to increase the amount of work that Rose carried out as a prostitute. They frequently placed advertisements in the back of adult magazines advertising her services. Accompanied by racy photos taken by Fred, the adverts served to suggest that Rose was ready and waiting for any business that might come her way. As ever, the children knew that when the red light was lit outside "Rose's Room," they were not allowed to enter.

Added to this, Fred and Rose began to host a number of sex parties in their home. Fred had installed a small bar in the house, naming it the "Black Magic Bar." Here, they would welcome people who had a similarly non-traditional interest in the world of sex. While the other people perhaps did not share Fred and West's murderous instinct, the parties were a way in which the couple could at least share some of their interests with people outside of the marriage. During these times, the children were still living in the home. Fred and Rose's daughters continued to suffer from a horrific childhood. With Anne-Marie and Heather increasingly of an age where they appealed to Fred's lusts, they were frequently raped by their father.

Lucy Partington was far removed from this world. She was a student at Exeter University, reading English Literature. Originally from St. Albans, she was the third child of Margaret and Roger Partington. On a break from her studies, she was spending her time away from university in Gloucester. We know that she was abducted some time on the night of December the 27th, 1974. In the two days after Christmas, Fred and Rose West had set out on the prowl to try and find another victim they could bend to their will. They came across Lucy. Picking her up from the road on her way home from the movies, she was likely tricked into getting into the car with the Wests, before she was lured into the home, bound, raped, and killed. The story takes a slightly different turn in that we know what happened to Fred in the new few days. Fred West was admitted to hospital after driving himself to the casualty unit on the 3rd of January. Once he arrived at Gloucester hospital, he was treated for a serious wound to his hand. He had a very large laceration along the right hand and needed a number of stitches to close it up.

Though we do not know the exact reason for the wound, we can speculate. With Lucy having been abducted only a few days earlier, it is possible that Fred and Rose were able to torture her while keeping her alive up until the 3rd January, eight days after the original disappearance. With their newfound ability to keep victims alive, it is possible that the couple had been torturing Lucy when something went wrong. Perhaps a misplaced item of cruelty slipped from Fred's hand when he was applying pain to the young girl. Perhaps Rose got carried away with her depravity and tried to inflict pain on her husband. Perhaps even Lucy managed to almost escape, and in slicing her way through Fred's hands did she nearly achieve her freedom only to be stopped by Rose. It might just have been a standard construction accident. We just don't know.

What Fred's injury does teach us about the Wests' crimes is that they were likely improving in their ability to torture and to keep their victims alive. It also demonstrates that despite the lessons they had learned, they were still prone to impulsive behavior and were not as bullet-proof as they might have previously considered themselves.

The last thing to note during the case of Lucy Partington is the manner in which the public responded to her death. When it became apparent that Lucy had been one of the victims of Fred and Rose West, there was a number of media pieces, memoirs, plays, and even books produced. After the couple was caught and the cellar excavated, Lucy's body was found. Her body, as was the case withal the West victims, had been dismembered. The knife that had been used to cut her apart was buried next to her. Following the investigation, Lucy's remains were taken away and buried in Exeter.

Perhaps appropriately for a girl who was studying English Literature and who was a distant cousin of the famous novel writer, Martin Amis, Lucy's death prompted the biggest artistic response. Her sister Marian published a memoir dealing about the way in which her sister vanished and how it affected the family. A great deal of the information was gleaned from Marian's writing in the Guardian newspaper where she had covered the topic in a series of articles. In turn, her works inspired a play written by Bryony Lavery, which was then made into a feature-length film by director Juliet McKoen. Both the play and the movie bore the title "Frozen." Of all the victims in this book, Lucy Partington's life after death is the one that has been most extensively covered.

Therese Siegenthaler and Shirley Hubbard

During the course of 1974, Fred and Rose West killed two more young girls. When looking through the cases of serial killers in recent history, there is often a pattern whereby they either work in bursts of short, sharp activity followed by long stretches of nothingness, or they accelerate rapidly through victims and are caught or killed in a short space of time. Fred and Rose West were different. Rather than feeling compelled to kill again and again, they managed to space out their attacks and to refrain from murdering as many young girls as they possibly could. The reason for this might have been the fact that Fred and Rose were able to get sexual gratification from other places. Rose had her string of clients as a prostitute (which still included her father) and was repeatedly pregnant during this time. Fred, conversely, enjoyed simply watching Rose with the various men who paid to have sex with her, while continuing to rape his daughters. Of the daughters, it was Anne-Marie and (later) Heather who would suffer the worst, most frequent abuse.

With the couple's focus being chiefly on selecting targets that they felt no one would miss, they discovered a whole new range of possibilities when they came across Therese Siegenthaler. Therese was originally from Switzerland and was in the country studying. Though she had been living in South London at the time of her disappearance, Fred and Rose picked her up while she was attempting to hitchhike her way to Ireland. Having had to pass through the Wests' Gloucester territory, she was unlucky enough to catch the couple in a murderous mood.

Being Swiss and far away from her home meant that there were few people keeping tabs on Therese. Because she had hitchhiked her way from South London and was close to halfway to her destination across the Irish Sea, few people actually knew where she was. For those who were aware of her methods of travel, the lack of mobile phones in the 1970s meant that she could have been anywhere between London and Dublin. That she was Swiss meant that she had fewer family members in Britain to lodge a complaint or notice her disappearance. When she went missing in April of 1974, there were few people who knew where she might be and fewer still who had the inclination to report her disappearance as being suspicious. Because of this, she was almost a perfect choice of victim for Fred and Rose. She was twenty-two at the time of her death.

With four months having passed between the abduction of Lucy Partington and the disappearance of Therese Siegenthaler, Fred and Rose demonstrated their ability to pick their targets in a more selective fashion. Rather than rushing out and finding the first girl on the street, they were cautious in their approach. Likewise, they waited another six months before they struck again. Unlike many serial killers, this spacing out of the victims allowed for the murderers to better cover their tracks and to ensure that they were not under suspicion at any point. While they may have been driven by their sadistic impulses, Fred and Rose were able to turn a calculating consideration on their actions. Perhaps because they were working in a pair, they were able to rein in the wild desires and carnal motivations that drive many mass-murderers and lead to so many being caught.

It was October of 1974 before they struck again. This time, they again decided to go for a teenage target. Shirley Hubbard was fifteen at the time of her death. Having been born on the 1st of March, 1957, she was only several years older than Charmaine had been at the time of her death. Shirley had been taking part in a work experience placement in Droitwich. The course was located some distance from her house, and the journey back and forth was long. One day, she simply did not arrive home. Though her parents were concerned and reported the matter to the police, there was little in the way of evidence. Shirley's name was added to the missing persons' register.

In actual fact, she had fallen prey to two of England's most dangerous people. After having picked up the young girl and offered her a lift home, Fred and Rose West whisked the teenager back to 25 Cromwell Street. When the bodies were eventually recovered by the investigators, Shirley's remains were slightly different. Where the others had been bound and gagged, Shirley had actually had her entire head covered in tape. Mummified, a small rubber tube had been shoved through the tape and into her mouth, allowing her to breath.

It is unknown how long Shirley was forced to endure this kind of existence. With her head completely tied up, she was unable to see, hear, move, or breathe in a normal fashion. Her captors' torture techniques were taking new turns. Not content with simply tying up, gagging, and raping the young girls, Fred and Rose were searching for new ways in which they could inflict all manner of pain on the victims. For Shirley, this meant sensory deprivation.

During this time, the girls who were killed continued to be buried underneath the cellar floor. These are the only victims who we know about. While Fred and Rose were charged only with the killings of those whose bodies were found across their numerous properties, detectives have not ruled out the possibility that other murders took place and the bodies buried elsewhere. Should this be the case, the Wests were far more careful with their body disposal methods than we might ever have expected.

Juanita "Nita" Marion Mott, Shirley Anne Robinson, and Alison Chambers

Keeping track of the murders of Fred and Rose West has been a difficult process. During the time they were embarking on their spree of murders, it seems as though they managed to restrain themselves and only killed on a semi-regular basis. From the late 1960s to the late 1970s, it seemed as though they averaged one murder each year. Some years saw multiple killings, while others saw none at all. Occupying themselves with various sexual pleasures, molestations, and incestuous rapes, Fred and Rose found other ways in which to pass the time. As we will see when Fred was finally arrested, the police believe that there might actually have been many more victims than those that were definitively attributed to the pair. Though the Fred and Rose West murders officially totaled ten women (that is, those they murdered as a pair,) Fred admitted to the police that they had actually killed many more. Due to the nature of these crimes and the lack of evidence, this book will only focus on the deaths which would eventually make up the bulk of the court case against Fred and Rose West. That is to say, the girls whom they murdered and buried in the cellar. Over the course of 1975, 1978, and 1979, the couple added three more victims to the official lists.

The first of these was Juanita Mott, known to her friends as "Nita." Like so many people who had passed through the West's home over the years, she had initially taken the room as a lodger. It is unclear whether she had any indication of the interests of Fred and Rose as they pertained to matters of a sexual nature, but she took the room regardless. She was last seen alive in April of 1975. By this time, she had already moved out of the home. Whether she had been turned off by a proposition by Fred or his wife or whether she had moved on of her own accord, we simply do not know. What we do know is that Fred and Rose sought her out once more after she had moved to a home in Newent where she was staying with one of her family's friends. Perhaps it happened like in the case of Caroline Owens, where Fred and Rose appeared to her and offered their apologies, citing a misunderstanding. Whatever method they used to trick her, Juanita was added to the long list of victims and was buried at 25 Cromwell Street after being tortured.

Following the death of Juanita Mott, Fred and Rose took it upon themselves to halt their killing for one of the longest periods since they began. Over the course of the next two years, they refrained from killing any young girls, at least those that we are aware of, and no more bodies were buried at the house. In terms of the constant burials that had been taking place, Fred had been forced to find an excuse for his work on the house. Toiling under the presence of home improvements, he was constantly telling neighbors of the repairs and the work that he was being forced to carry out. They bought the story, providing an excellent excuse for the work with which Fred would hide away the remnants of the girls killed by the Wests.

As well as needing an excuse to cover up the building work that was happening at 25 Cromwell Street, Fred also needed supplies. Not a rich man, having to invest in the DIY tools and building materials was beginning to take its toll. To get around this, Fred began to take part in a series of thefts. Taking goods from all across the area, he would sell them for cheap and keep the money. This would be reinvested in the "home improvements" in his house. While the thefts were at least enough to warrant semi-regular attention from the police, this attention was never enough to uncover his string of murders, nor the incestuous rape he was still regularly committing.

During this time, his abuse led to a rather serious issue. Anne-Marie West, his legitimate daughter from his first marriage, was one of his primary targets for rape. At this time, she became pregnant with Fred's daughter. While he wondered how to deal with the situation, it became clear that the baby would need to be terminated for medical reasons. Following the loss of the pregnancy, Anne-Marie finally left home. As such, Fred's attentions turned elsewhere. His next primary target was Heather, born in 1970. As she grew older, Fred grew more and more interested, and the rapes grew more and more frequent. There have been suggestions that Heather might not have been Fred's daughter. At the time of her conception, as well as for long periods before and after, Rose's father continued to visit her and have sex while Fred watched. After a childhood in which she was abused by her parents, Rose had started to charge her father for sex under the guidance of her husband. According to some investigators, Heather was the child of Rose and her father. Along with Heather, Fred also showed an interest in one of his legitimate daughter, Mae, whom he also raped.

At the end of 1975, it became clear that Fred's plan of burying people in the cellar was not a long-term solution. With the bodies starting to take up too much space – and with the couple having a break from murdering people – Fred switched his attentions elsewhere. The cellar was renovated. The room where he had tortured, raped, killed, and buried a series of teenage girls was covered in concrete. After this, Fred turned the cellar into a playroom for his children. When the police eventually arrived to dig up the bodies, they found that the room had been painted with childish murals to make it seem like a happier place for the younger kids. Pictures of clowns and cowboys had been painted along the walls. Beneath the murals, police dug down to discover the bodies.

Despite taking a short sabbatical from the murder spree, Fred and Rose could never entirely separate themselves from the idea of torturing and killing people. As such, when faced with a problem in their life, they once again turned to the sadistic in order to both solve their issues and to indulge their own fantasies. When they met a woman named Shirley Anne Robinson, they likely had little idea that their murderous intentions would be rekindled after almost three years.

Shirley was nineteen when she first arrived at the Wests household. Though they were spending less and less time looking for active targets and more time raising their children, Fred and Rose were still taking in lodgers. When a young girl arrived on their doorstep looking for somewhere to live, they found it difficult to say no. Instead, they welcomed her into their home. Still working as a prostitute, Shirley quickly found out about the manner of the West's lifestyle and their interests in the less traditional aspects of sex.

It was not long before Shirley was herself working as a prostitute. Likely falling under the manipulative influence of Fred, she was soon taking in clients of her own and joining Rose in the sex industry. Not only this, but she occasionally found herself working directly for Fred and Rose, paid to have sex and engage in their less twisted indulgences. This lasted for a short amount of time. As ever with Fred and Rose, however, it was not long before they was turning their minds towards more murderous intentions.

The fatal moment arrived when Shirley discovered that she was pregnant. Now carrying Fred's baby, she was suddenly in a very vulnerable position. Not only was Fred less than keen to welcome yet another illegitimate daughter into the world, but the arrival of the pregnancy also rekindled in Rose the jealous urges that had driven her to kill Charmaine many years ago. Now carrying a death sentence inside her, Shirley's fate was sealed.

While Fred had once boasted of all the women for whom her had performed abortions, both he and Rose chose not to simply terminate the pregnancy. Instead, they returned to their sadistic worst. Shirley was eighteen in May 1978, the time when the Wests eventually turned on her. They faced a problem in that the cellar was no longer available to them as a placed in which they could store the remains. Once they had raped, tortured, and killed the young girl, they had to find a new place to dispose of the body. They turned to the garden.

Fred and Rose had recently decided to renovate the outside areas of their home. In their small back garden, they installed a patio. Lifting up the paving slabs once more, Fred returned to his usual method of dismembering the body and burying it in a shallow grave beneath the thick concrete slabs. Covering it back up quickly, few of the neighbors even noticed.

Now that they had gotten the taste for murder back, it was not nearly as long before Fred and Rose felt the need to kill again. Their next victim was Alison Chambers. She is widely regarded as the last of the West victims to have been killed due to a predominantly sexual motivation. Following the murder of Shirley Robinson, Fred and Rose returned to their normal lives (as far in as an incestuous, abusive household can be considered normal). It would be just over a year before they turned their attentions one more to the prospect of murdering a young girl.

Alison Chambers was born in 1962 on the 8th of September. At the time of her death, she was sixteen and a day away from her seventeenth birthday. Like so many others before her, she was a young girl in a vulnerable position. When Fred and Rose first approached her, they seemed to be offering a helping, friendly hand. It was all just part of a great act. By now, they had become so practiced that they were able to manipulate, seduce, and abuse teenage girls almost without thinking.

And just like so many before her, Alison Chambers was taken back to 25 Cromwell Street. While hidden from the children, Fred and Rose bound and gagged the girl. They tortured and raped her over a number of days before eventually - finally - killing her. Once again, Fred returned to the outdoor areas of his home and dug up the patio. Working under the cover of night, he lifted enough of the slabs and dug down far enough that he could fit the young girl's body underneath. Before dawn, he had successfully hidden the corpse from the attentions of his neighbors. Once again, it seemed as though Fred and Rose had gotten away with murder.

After the death of Alison Chambers, Fred and Rose stopped in their efforts to kill teenage girls. At the very least, they stopped burying the bodies in Cromwell Street. While it is heavily suspected that Fred and Rose killed many more people than they let on, we simply have no method of separating the long lists of missing women from those who mate their tragic end at the hands of the Wests before being buried elsewhere. There would be one more body buried at 25 Cromwell Street. It would be the one which would lead directly to the couple finally being caught.

Heather Ann West

For the next eight years, Fred and Rose kept themselves relatively low-key. Though we do not have the evidence required to attribute any murders to them at this time, that is not to say that they spent their time in an innocent fashion. Far from it. In the lead-up to 1987, Fred had been focusing his attentions more and more on his daughter, Heather Ann West. Since the departure of Anne-Marie, Heather had emerged as the chosen target of her father's incestuous affections. Throughout all of the physical, emotional, and sexual abuse she suffered, she had kept quiet. As we have previously covered in this book, there was a high likelihood that Heather was not, in fact, Fred's daughter. Instead, she was possibly the results of Rose and her father's frequent sexual encounters. Perhaps because of this, his abuse focused more on Heather than any of the other girls under his care.

Few of Fred's daughters escaped his attentions, nor was Rose an innocent party in the abuse. With both emerging from childhoods in which incestuous abuse had played a part in the household, the prospect of in-family rape was not unfamiliar to either. For Rose, she had been having sex with her father for a number of years, encouraged by Fred. With this in mind, the West children were raised in an abusive environment that is almost impossible to envisage. With all of the female children in danger of being raped by Fred whenever he felt the urge, Rose focused on the emotional and psychological abuse of the children and ensured that they were always kept in their place by restricting their freedoms, their means of expression, and being sure to diminish, beat, and mistreat them at every turn. Even on those occasions when there was a nanny in the household, both Fred and Rose took the time to ensure that their children were constantly abused and mistreated.

This came to a head in June of 1987. By this time, Heather had grown into a sixteen-year-old girl. Allowed to leave the house, she had built up a small group of trusted friends. After decades of abuse in the West household, Fred and Rose began to get the feeling that their daughter might confide in her friends the fact that her father had been abusing her and her sisters for as long as she could remember. This had already happened once in June of 1986, a year before, but nothing had come of it. Not wanting to risk the possibility that Heather might alert the authorities, Fred and Rose decided that something must be done about their daughter. They hatched a plan.

It was later claimed by Fred that he had never meant to kill Heather. It was his claim that she had "sneered" in his direction and his intention was merely to discipline her. In his words, he sought to take the smile off her face. Regardless of what he later told the police, the death seemed to have been planned ahead. After sending the other children off to school, Fred and Rose kept Heather behind. Once they were alone with their daughter, Fred struck. He wrapped his arms around the girl's throat and strangled her.

Once she was dead, Heather's body was added to the others underneath the patio. Talking to a neighbor the next day, Rose told of the "awful row" she had had with her daughter and apologized for all of the noise they had made. The conversation drove home the fact that the Wests would need a cover story when asked about their missing little girl, not only by the neighbors, but by their other children. To the remainder of the West children, the story was that Heather had departed for a job in Devon, allegedly leaving to take up a position at a holiday camp. For the neighbors, the story took a more tabloid turn. They told people that she had run away to be with her lesbian lover.

But the story was not always enough. While the neighbors seemed happy enough to buy into the story, the children in the West household seemed to have their own suspicions.

The idea that Heather was in Devon was seemingly known to be a lie. To this extent, Fred even joked around with the remaining children, telling them that – should they fail to behave correctly and keep quiet – they would end up under the patio just like their sister.

When looking back over the death of Heather West, Dr. David Holmes has noted the delicate position that Heather had placed the family into. Had she talked, he believes, the entire murderous façade was in danger of tumbling down. Her continued existence could not be tolerated. In effect, Dr. Holmes believed that the risky nature of the murder even served to provide a threat to the other children, warning them of the dangers of potentially talking to the police about their parents' activities.

In this respect, the death of Heather West seemed as though it was an essential move on behalf of the Wests. With their daughter threatening to expose their abusive behaviors, attention in this regard could have proven to lead to their history of torture and murder. As it turned out, it would be the first steps towards their undoing. What they had originally seen as being perhaps the only essential murder of their spree would eventually be the one that brought about their downfall.

The Investigation

Following the death of Heather West, rumors began to worm their way around the local community. Despite the Wests' protestations about Heather having run away with her lesbian lover, her absence was noted in numerous circles. Despite these persistent rumors spreading through the town, it was not until 1992 that Fred or Rose encountered any actual repercussions.

Following the death of Heather, Fred and Rose enjoyed a complete authoritarian control over their children. Both the boys and the girls in the house had noted the absence of their sister. Added in were the occasional jokes made by their father about what might happen to them should they disobey his orders. Throughout this time, Fred continued to sexually abuse the girls in the household, and Rose continued to allow him to do so, while occasionally watching and assisting in the abuse. In May of 1992, a leap forward in technology would provide Fred with a new titillation and a new avenue down which he would incriminate himself.

That May, Fred had acquired a video camera. The new toy allowed him to film whatever caught his fancy and meant that he could record moments that he found to be particularly interesting. For a serial abuser and rapist, this inevitably meant that he chose to film the sordid rape of his daughters. Just as was the case with Heather five years earlier, one their abused daughters felt compelled to tell her friends and to seek out a sympathetic ear after years and years of abuse. For the first time, there was physical evidence to back up the claims made by one of the girls and to ratify the rumors which had spread about what happened inside 25 Cromwell Street.

After having told a group of friends about the rapes, one of the friends decided to take the matter very seriously and told her mother who went to the police. Fred was known to the person who took up the lead investigator role on the matter. An investigating officer named Hazel Savage, she had known Fred back from the time when he was married to Catherine Costello. The word of an investigation spread around the town, enough that another girl got the courage to come forward. She too had been raped by Fred West (though was not one of his daughters). After having two separate indications of Fred's crimes, the police gathered together a search warrant and made their way to the house.

In August of 1992, the police went through the home to find any evidence that might provide a conviction. After searching through the house on Cromwell Street, they believed that they had enough evidence to convict Fred and charged him with sodomy of a minor and rape. These were serious charges, with Rose being arrested at the same time as an accomplice. While their parents were taken away and processed by the authorities, the children were out from under their parents' care for the first time in their lives. They were taken in and placed under government care.

Following the processing, Fred was taken into custody. Rose, conversely, was released and even allowed to see her children once again. During this time, she became notably depressed. Without Fred and concerned about their future and whether they would be caught for their crimes, she even attempted to commit suicide. She was halted during the act by one of her sons.

Despite the wealth of evidence that was available – including two testimonies – the case against Fred fell apart. The victims seemed unwilling to come forward and press charges against the man. The police had no choice but to release him. He returned to the household with Rose, and the children were returned to their parents' care. But for Detective Constable Savage, this was not the end of the matter. Convinced that there was more to the case than met the eye, she refused to give up on the possibility that Fred and Rose West had something to hide.

Following Fred's release, Detective Savage began to review the evidence. She looked into the disappearance of Heather and could find no corroborating evidence for the parents' story. She examined the transcripts of the interviews given by the West children following the arrest of Fred and Rose. Buried deep inside were confessions that their father had threatened to bury them under the patio, just like their older sister. Asking throughout the community and reviewing the past case files against the couple, she finally felt that she had enough of a suspicion to warrant a second search of the home.

The whole process took two years. In 1994, the police returned to 25 Cromwell Street with a second warrant. Fred was taken into custody, and the police began to search through the home. Unfortunately, they had no real idea where they should be looking. With the basement concreted over, the remaining bodies were hidden beneath the patio. As the police searched, they walked back and forth over the place where a number of women had been dismembered and buried, just above the fish pond that Stephen West had once dug and that his father had then filled in.

Luckily for the police, they did not have to search too hard. At the police station, the questioning of Fred West led to him finally breaking down and confessing his crimes. As he told the investigators, the bodies were buried beneath the patio. He admitted to murdering his daughter. During the search for Heather, the police came across an increasing number of bones. Still at the police station, Fred began to admit to an ever-increasing number of murders. He took sole responsibility for the deaths, refusing to implicate Rose. Even in this circumstance, he wished to protect her.

Despite the bodies and bones being turned up, Fred refused to admit that he had raped any of the women. Instead, he told the police that each of the women had willingly had sex with him. Looking back over his past addresses and actions, the police soon turned up the bodies of Anne McFall and Charmaine West. Desperate to protect herself from being prosecuted, Rose suddenly cut off all ties to her husband. She pretended to be as surprised as everyone else.

It would be April before the police decided that they had enough evidence to arrest Rose as well. The initial charges focused on the sex offences she had committed, but the scope was widened to murder as the evidence began to mount. On the 30th of June, the pair were held up before a magistrate's court and told that they were being charged with murder. The final count was twelve for Fred and ten for Rose.

Finally, Fred and Rose West had been caught. After decades of abuse, torture, rape, and murder, they had finally come to the attention of the authorities. With the trial set to start in the coming weeks, they had become a national sensation. As more and more bodies were pulled out of the house at 25 Cromwell Street, the public was appalled and fascinated in equal measure. The case took over the television news and the print media. At this point, Fred was still seeking to protect the love of his life. He refused to suggest that Rose had been complicit in any of the murders and tried to take full responsibility. Rose, for her part, stuck to this story. Even in court, she refused to accept that she had been anything other than a pawn in her husband's murderous plans. With the public calling for justice, there was still one twist in the tale.

The Aftermath

Fred West was imprisoned in Winson Green while he awaited trial. His Birmingham Prison cell was one of the best guarded in the country and the focus of a huge amount of attention. Fred, his psychological condition considered to be perilous, was placed on suicide watch. Despite this, Fred West hanged himself on the 1st of January, 1995. Stringing together a number of bedsheets, he placed the noose around his neck and allowed it strangle him to death. He was cremated nearly three months later, and only four people turned up at his funeral. It was a private, five-minute service, after which his ashes were scattered on the beach in Barry Island, Wales. He had escaped being tried and convicted of the murders but had admitted to carrying out far more than the police were able to attest to. In death, he escaped his punishment.

For Rose, suicide was not an option. Still protesting her innocence, she knew the evidence against her was far less convincing. She had not confessed to the murders. Despite this, Rose was found guilty of all ten murders in October of 1995. The trial was a sensation in the media, and the press were quick to label her as one of history's most evil women. Without her husband by her side, she took the brunt of the public's blame for the murders.

After a long trial and a huge amount of interest, the judge recommended that Rose West never be released from jail.

After two years of political movement back and forth, the then-Home Secretary, Jack Straw, agreed with this decision and handed out a tariff for life imprisonment. At the time, Rose was only the second woman to receive such a punishment, the first being Myra Hindley some years earlier.

In January of 1996, the case took another strange turn. One of the Wests' former lodgers and a man who considered himself to be a friend of the family was found dead in his car. Terrence Crick was discovered in his vehicle in Hackness. He had been one of the defense's key witnesses at Rose's trial, with his testimony being used to demonstrate to the jury that Fred had been solely responsible. His account included stories about the times that Fred would come to him with a number photographs, all of which showed variously gruesome parts of the body in differing states, accompanied by images of surgical instruments. Fred told him that these were the tools he used to perform abortions. It was found that Crick had killed himself, undone by the pressure, the stress, and the guilt that came with being associated with Rose West.

The home where Fred and Rose killed and buried their victims became notorious across Britain. Still remembered today, the cellar and the patio of 25 Cromwell Street have become part of popular culture and the myth of the country's serial killers. Rather than selling it to another person, the house was demolished. It was positioned next to another home and a church, but was simply knocked down and a pathway built on top of it. To discourage people from seeking out mementos, every single brick was demolished and crushed, while every piece of timber was burned.

Because of Fred West's suicide and because of the fact that Rose West continues to deny her role in the murders to this day, it is hard to tell what exactly she did to the girls who were buried in the basement, as well as to the many more whose remains may be scattered across the countryside and as yet unfound. We do know that – before Rose met her future husband – Fred was already a rapist and a murderer. Added to this, he was willing to take full responsibility for the crimes, and it was only after his death that Rose grew into such a key figure in the case. However, we do have the account from Caroline Owens, which paints Rose as not only a complicit part of a rape and torture scenario, but as someone who actively enjoyed it and encouraged it in her partner. With this in mind, added to the tales of abuse and neglect that come from her children, it can be safe to say that Rose West was indeed an active participant in many of the murders. As such, her guilty conviction was correct.

Ever since the close of the trial, there have been a number of theories bandied about which attempt to fill in the missing gaps in the story. Some have suggested that rather than kill all of the girls at the house on Cromwell Street, the Wests actually murdered their victims elsewhere and simply buried the bodies at their home. Others have put forward the suggestions that the real reason for Fred and Rose's killings was as part of a wider series of satanic rituals, though there is little evidence that supports this notion. Certain theories claim to have knowledge of the location of the unknown victims and purport to know where the bodies are buried. Such locations have included abandoned farm houses, fields, and roadsides. Again, however, there is little evidence to back up these claims, other than the circumstantial.

In terms of the motivation of killers, we do know that the majority of serial killers, whose profiles have been studied by investigators, come from abusive backgrounds. Both Fred and Rose were raised in households where abuse was a major occurrence. Similarly, many killers have reportedly suffered from serious head injuries in their youth, which is again true of Fred. As he grew older, the fantasies and desires that came into Fred's mind became increasingly sadistic. Bondage was an early obsession, with immobile and helpless partners being of central attraction to his carnal wishes. Starting as a rapist and becoming increasingly interested in torture, the victims found themselves similarly bound while their attacker carried out his fantasies. Terror and pain accompanied this bondage until they became a prime motivation and an essential part of the act. Always seeking to extend his pleasure, the methods of binding, torturing, and mutilating his victims became increasingly more refined and complicated. From an early childhood, Fred West's horrific acts can be traced along a line as they became increasingly more depraved. By the time he killed himself, he had done more than enough to earn a place among the most sadistic and cruel serial killers in criminal history.

But what of Rose West? As the surviving partner in the murderous couple, she became the face of the West killings. Without her husband to take some of the blame in the press, she became the lightning rod for the media's demonization process. Not without reason, she became quickly known as one of the most evil women in history. To this day, she still lives in prison and is regularly mentioned in the press. Stories abound in the British press, telling readers about her exploits behind bars. Some paint her as a woman who swaps knitting patterns and recipes with other inmates and even as a person who has struck up a long-lasting relationship with a fellow prisoner. Others depict West as a paranoid arch-criminal, cutting her own hair out of fear of being stabbed while ordering attacks on other inmates and overseeing a network of underlings. With such a monstrous figure, it is almost impossible to get a modern-day handle on the character of Rose West, other than the lasting legacy that her killings and trial left behind. For many people in Britain, she is the face of evil.

Conclusion

Though not well known around the world, the story of Fred and Rose West contains all of the classic hallmarks of the highest profile serial killer cases around. The involvement of two people in this instance marks it out as different from cases such as John Wayne Gacy or Jeffrey Dahmer. In terms of the history of serial killers, there is almost a Bonnie and Clyde element to their actions, but with the couple torturing, murdering, raping, and abusing their own children instead of robbing banks.

If you have read through this book, then you will have discovered the full extent to which evil can corrupt, infect, and take over the lives of two people. That they raised a family and brought a large number of children into the situation adds just another tragic element to the tale. For the murderers' girls and the abused West children, this is a horrific and terrible tale. For the rest of us, it is the chance to see inside the minds of not one, but two of the most evil people in modern history.

Further Reading

Bennett, John (2005). *The Cromwell Street Murders: The Detective's Story*. Sutton Publishing.

Burn, Gordon (1998). *Happy Like Murderers*. London: Faber and Faber.

Carter Woodrow, Jane (2011). *Rose West: The making of a Monster*. Hodder & Stoughton (UK).

Masters, Brian (1996). *She Must Have Known: Trial of Rosemary West*. London: Doubleday.

Roberts, Caroline (2005). *The Lost Girl: How I Triumphed Over Life at the Mercy of Fred and Rose West*. London: Metro Books.

Sounes, Howard (1995). *Fred and Rose: The Full Story of Fred and Rose West and the Gloucester House of Horrors*. London: Warner Books.

Wansell, Geoffrey (1996). *An Evil Love: The Life of Frederick West*. London: Hodder Headline.

West, Anne Marie (1995). *Out of the Shadows: Fred West's Daughter Tells Her Harrowing Story of Survival*. Simon & Schuster.

Wilson, Colin (1998). *The Corpse Garden*. London: True Crime Library.

Partington, Marian (2012). *If You Sit Very Still*. Vala Publishing Co-operative.

Confirmed Murders Timeline

Charmaine West - Killed in June, 1971.

Catherine Bernadette "Rena" West - Killed August, 1971.

Lynda Gough - Killed April, 1973.

Carol Ann Cooper - Killed November, 1973.

Lucy Katherine Partington - Killed December, 1973.

Theresa Siegenthaler - Killed in April, 1974.

Shirley Hubbard - Killed November, 1974.

Juanita Marion Mott - Killed April, 1975.

Shirley Anne Robinson - Killed May, 1978.

Alison Chambers - Killed August, 1979.

Heather Ann West – Killed June, 1987.

Presumed killed but no body was found to date

Mary Bastholm – presumed killed in January 1968

Excerpt of Jack Smith's Book Serial Killers Volume 2 Exploring the Horrific True Crimes of Little Known Murderers

Serial killers are big business. From the endless books, films, and television programs to the fascination of the twenty-four-hour news networks, there is something about these mass murderers that catches the eye and the attention. While many people are familiar with better-known killers like John Wayne Gacy or Jack the Ripper, they are not the whole story. There are so many examples of serial killers from around the world that many of them have simply been forgotten.

That does not make their crimes any less serious. Instead, some of these serial killers committed heinous acts above and beyond those we have come to expect when thinking about the worst psychopaths in living memory. In cases such as these, the truth is often stranger than fiction. For every Hannibal Lecter or Norman Bates, the murders committed by the people detailed in this book are often more extreme, violent, and off-putting than anything you might find in fiction.

As we delve further and further into the book, we will begin to see not only the extremities of the crimes, but also the difficulty the authorities face when trying to catch a killer. With so many serial killers on the record books of human history, it is a wonder that we have caught as many as we have. Even in the cases where no one has ever been arrested for the crimes, we can learn a lot about the mind sets of the individuals involved. As we travel further into the minds of the forgotten serial killers, we will not only learn more about what turns people into violent mass murderers, but we will also learn how these individuals are shaped and treated by society. The morbid fascination we have with serial killers is matched only by the violence of the crimes in question. Read on and find out more about history's forgotten serial killers.

The son of a candy factory owner who carried out the Houston Mass Murders

Dean Corll

The Candy Man' or 'The Pied Piper'

Where: USA
When: 1970-1973
Number of victims: 28 and more

Background

Dean Arnold Corll was one of America's worst serial killers. His killing spree during the 1970s was to be one of the most violent and worrying that the country had faced up to that point. His propensity to prey on children made his crimes all the more notorious. With deaths reaching almost thirty, it was perhaps the enlisting of two young accomplices that made people take note of the extreme manipulation and violence that was being carried out. Coupled with this, the lack of a true trial and punishment has led to there being a sense of unresolved justice about the case. But who exactly was Corll?

Growing up, Dean's father was very strict on the boy. But as the first born son, Dean was treated quite the opposite byhis mother. She took an overbearing and overprotective approach to raising the child. This split between the ways the parents treated their son was reflected in other aspects of their relationship. Frequently quarrelling and often fighting, the parents lost their marriage – possibly inevitably – as it ended in divorce in 1946. By this time, Dean was close to seven years old. Dean's mother, Mary, took the children and moved into a trailer in Memphis, Tennessee. The location was chosen so that the boys would have frequent chances to see their father, who had been drafted into the air force and was serving nearby. Following the breakup of the marriage, there would be a number of attempts to reconcile the relationship.

Dean Corll was always affected by his environment. As a shy boy, he had little contact with children his own age. Despite this, there have been numerous accounts that recall the ways in which he demonstrated great empathy and sympathy for others and attempted to help them. His childhood would be affected by illness when an undiagnosed bout of rheumatic fever led to the doctors discovering that Dean had a heart murmur. Because of this, he was excluded from many of the more physical activities at his school.

Thankfully, 1950 would prove to be a more hopeful year for the family. Renewing their marriage, Dean's parents packed up the family and moved to Texas. This marriage would last only three years, however, and the couple once again divorced. Mary took custody of the children, and again she wanted them to be near their father following a fairly amicable divorce. She would marry another man shortly after, a travelling clock salesman who encouraged the family to move to Vidor. This would be the place where Dean's family would open a candy store. Named "Pecan Prince," it started as a small experiment in their home before growing far larger. For the young boys, they were given the task of operating the machinery for making the candy. This was then sold by their stepfather during his normal sales routes. They grew more popular than they might ever have imagined.

After a complicated childhood, Dean graduated with reasonable grades. Always regarded as something of a loner, he had intermittent relationships with a number of girls. It was noted that his only real hobby was the high school band, in which he played trombone. By the time he left school, the Corll family business was booming. The family relocated to larger premises outside of Houston to expand the business. Dean would spend two years away from Houston, moving to Indiana to care for his sick grandmother. When he returned to Houston, his mother's recent divorce made her form her own business, the Corll Candy Company. Dean was made president. This was interrupted in 1964, when he was drafted for military service. During an unblemished spell, he served for ten months and was said to have hated it. While in the military, he had his first encounters of a homosexual nature. The lasting effect, as he later told friends, was to help him realize that he was homosexual.

After being honorably discharged from the armed forces, Dean returned to his position as Vice President. The firm was running into stiff competition from Dean's former stepfather, and the two companies battled one another for market share. The Corll Candy Company moved to a bigger premises in Houston to meet demand, opening a factory opposite an elementary school. Here, Dean was known to hand out free samples of candy to the local children. This practice would later lead to his nickname, the Candy Man. Some even took to calling him the Pied Piper. Reports seemed to indicate that Dean would occasionally flirt with the male employees of the company, though these advances were usually rebuffed. The company installed a pool table at the rear of the factory that became a popular gathering spot for young males.

In 1967, Dean would meet a twelve-year-old named David Brooks. David Brooks would play a key role in this story. Often hanging around boys older than he was, David would spend time in the Corll Company's pool room. He took the free candy from Dean, and the two struck up a bond. Along with numerous other teenage boys, Dean and David would take regular trips to the seaside. Dean provided David with money when he was lacking and became a kind of substitute version of a father figure in the young boy's life. From here, at the regular urging of Dean Corll, the two entered into a sexual relationship. For various sexual acts, Dean Corll would pay the young boy money. But the arrangement did not last. David's parents divorced, and he moved seventy five miles away with his mother. On regular visits back to Houston, he would visit both his father and Dean. After a short while away, David dropped out of high school and moved back to Houston. By this time, he had come to regard Corll's home as his own.

The family business was not prospering, however. The Corll Candy Company closed in 1968, with Mary moving away to Colorado. Though she would speak with her son on the phone, they would never see one another again.

To make ends meet, Dean took on a job as an electrician. His crime wave would begin shortly after.

His crimes

Dean Corll's crimes began in 1970. During a period of three years, he is thought to have killed at least twenty-eight victims and likely more. The majority of these victims were young boys aged between thirteen and twenty. He preyed on one particular area, Houston Heights, abducting boys from this location and taking them away. At the time, Houston Heights was not a prosperous area. To help him achieve his violent visions, Corll employed the help of two young boys; David Brooks and Elmer Henley. He would prey on the friends of his accomplices or set his sights on other boys whom he had spotted around town. He would get to know the victims before abducting them. Some of them were even former employees of the family business.

To better get away with his murders, Corlls used a pair of vehicles. He owned both a Ford van and a Plymouth car, with a favorite trick being to offer a young boy a lift in either vehicle before simply driving away. Often, he would ply his victims with drugs or alcohol, making them pass out or become dazed enough that he might be able to fit them with handcuffs. Others he would simply grab using brute strength. Once he had them where he wanted them, Corll would strip his victims naked and tie them to either his bed or a specially constructed torture device that he had made from wooden boards. He would hang this device on the wall, leaving the boys manacled and unable to escape. Once trapped, Corll would begin a prolonged period of torture. This would involve them being beaten, sexually assaulted, and finally, killed. Sometimes they would be strangled to death, other times they would be shot with a small pistol.

Once deceased, they were wrapped in plastic sheeting and taken to one of four burial spots. These were a boat shed Corll had rented, a distant beach, a wooded area near a family cabin he owned, and another beach near Jefferson County. In an attempt to distract distraught parents from tracking down their children, Corll would often try and forge messages from the boys. He might have them phone their parents or write a letter saying not to come looking. Every now and again, he would take a trophy from his victims. These were found after his death. At this time in his life, staying in one location seemed like a bad idea. As such, Dean Corll moved from town to town quite frequently but remained in and around the Houston area.

The first known murder committed by Dean Corll was an eighteen-year-old named Jeffrey Konen. Killed in September of 1970, he vanished while travelling with another student from the University of Texas to a home in Houston belonging to his parents. It is thought that Corll, who lived in the area, offered a lift to Konen, who accepted. The body would not be discovered for three years, not until David Brooks led police officers to the scene. It had been buried on a beach, and investigators were able to determine that Jeffrey had died of asphyxiation. The body was not just buried. It had been hidden beneath a large bolder, covered by a small amount of lime and wrapped in plastic. The body was naked and tied at the hands at feet.

Around the same time that Jeffrey Konen had been murdered, David Brooks discovered the extent of Corll's crimes. He walked in on Dean Corll in the act of torturing two boys whom he had strapped to a plywood board. Corll bought Brooks's silence. He offered him a car in exchange for remaining quiet. Brooks received a Chevrolet Corvette for remaining silent on the subject. After this, Corll offered him two hundred dollars for every boy who he could lure to the apartment. Brooks accepted.

The first time Brooks was involved in the murders was in December of 1970. Two boys – both mutual acquaintances of Brooks – were lured into Corll's apartment. Dean Corll tied them up, strapped them to his torture boards, raped, and strangled them. He buried the boys in a boat shed. Over the coming months, Brooks would be a participant in many more murders. They would all follow the same pattern, with Brooks helping Corll lure the unsuspecting boys into trouble before Corll tortured and killed them. In these cases, the parents would often launch huge searches for their missing boys. These would often involve poster campaigns to try and garner any additional information. One of the boys paid to hand out these fliers was named Wayne Henley, who was fifteen years old.

Elmer Wayne Henley was introduced to Dean Corll by David Brooks. While it is initially thought that he had been lured to the apartment as an intended victim, Corll saw something in the boy that changed his mind. He offered the same deal to Henley as he had to Brooks; two hundred dollars for every boy successfully tricked into the apartment. Corll informed the young Henley that he was part of a sexual slavery ring operating in the area. While Henley did not accept at first, the poor finances of his family led him to take up the offer in 1972. The luring of boys would follow a similar pattern, with both Brooks and Henley working in tandem to attract victims to Corll's home.

Over the next year, Corll began to kill more and more people. Fully aware of the fate of the boys that they lured to the apartment, Henley and Brooks continued to work for the serial killer. It is thought that deaths were recorded on a scale of almost one a month all around Houston, with Corll frequently moving apartment and escaping detection. This would come to a head when he moved to a residence on Lamar Drive.

It was noted by both Brooks and Henley that Corll's move to this address prompted an upturn in the frequency and the brutality of the killings. At this point, both of the accomplices could tell when Corll felt in need of killing again. He would become agitated, would chain smoke, and would fritter and move chiefly on reflexes. At these times, he would tell them that he "needed to do a new boy." The attacks were only interspersed by a matter of days. This was despite the fact that David Brooks had taken a break from the crime spree to marry his pregnant girlfriend. The last victim, a boy of thirteen named James Dreymala, was abducted by both Brooks and Corll while on a bike ride. Like the others, he was strapped to the torture board, raped, and strangled to death before being buried.

Punishment

Punishment would not arrive in the conventional form. While many serial killers are eventually caught and prosecuted to the fullest extent of the law, Dean Corll's downfall began like many of his killings. On the 7th of August, 1973, Henley began to work toward luring a nineteen-year-old named Timothy Kerley back to Dean Corll's apartment. Together, the pair drank and sniffed paint fumes. Brooks was not involved in this instance. The pair met up with a fifteen-year-old girl named Rhonda Williams, who was currently hiding to escape her abusive, drunken father. Henley invited them all to Corll's apartment, where they arrived at three in the morning.

Upon arrival, Corll was furious that Henley had bought "a girl" to his home. He informed Henley that this would ruin everything. Henley tried to placate Corll, and it appeared to work, with the host then offering the teenagers beer and drugs. They partook and began to party for the next two hours, at which point they passed out.

Henley awoke to find himself being tied up by Dean Corll. The murderer was still furious that he had invited Rhonda to the home and was taping his accomplice's hands and feet together. Already bound, the other teenagers were lying beside Henley. Kerley had already been stripped of his clothes. Noticing that his one-time accomplice was waking up, Corll came across to talk, removing the gag. He informed Henley of his anger at Rhonda's arrival and, as such, he was going to kill all three of them. While explaining this, he repeatedly kicked Rhonda in the chest. To demonstrate his seriousness, he picked up Henley and dragged him into the kitchen, where he placed a pistol to his chest.

Henley begged for his life. He promised to help kill the others. Corll finally agreed and went back into the main room. Here, he began to fasten Kerley to the torture board and demanded that Henley do the same to Rhonda. Handing his young accomplice a hunting knife, the killer told him to remove her clothes and get started. While Kerley writhed in agony, Rhonda turned to Henley and asked whether this was all real. After he had confirmed it as such, she simply asked him whether he was going to do anything about it.

Having second thoughts, Henley asked whether he could take Rhonda into another room. He was ignored. Henley reacted by grabbing the pistol and screaming at Corll, telling Corll that he had gone too far this time. Henley said he would not stand by any longer while all his friends were killed. Corll advanced on him. He told Henley to shoot him, daring him to pull the trigger. Henley backed off. Corll laughed and told Henley that he would never be able to do it. Henley pulled the trigger. He shot Dean Corll in the forehead, but the bullet bounced off the man's skull. Corll lurched forward, and Henley shot him again. And again. Hit in the shoulder, Corll stumbled out of the room, but Henley chased him and shot him as he walked down the stairs. Dean Corll died then and there, naked and covered in blood.

Henley ran back into the room and freed the teenagers. They debated what to do before Henley resolved to call the police. He phoned them and confessed to the shooting. At the station, when being questioned about just the death of Dean Corll, he admitted to his role in the other killings. After a period of disbelief, he offered to take the police to see the bodies. They travelled out to the boat shed, where many bodies were found in various states of decay. After being called in by the police, David Brooks also gave a full confession. The pair helped the police recover the bodies. At the time, it was the highest body count for an American serial killer.

While Dean Corll had died, both David Brooks and Elmer Wayne Henley were tried for their role in the deaths. Both men were found guilty and are serving life sentences for their roles in helping one of America's most violent, prolific, and sadistic mass murderers.

More Books from Jack Smith

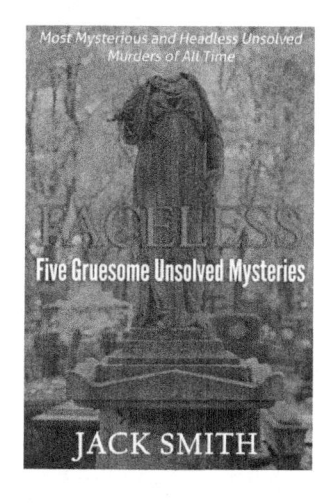

SERIAL
KILLERS
EXPLORING
THE HORRIFIC
CRIMES OF
LITTLE KNOWN
MURDERERS
JACK SMITH

SERIAL
KILLERS
VOL. 2
EXPLORING
THE HORRIFIC
TRUE CRIMES OF
LITTLE KNOWN
MURDERERS
JACK SMITH

WRONGFUL
CONVICTIONS
TRUE MURDER CASES
UNBELIEVABLE MISCARRIAGES OF JUSTICE
JACK SMITH

BY PERSON
OR PERSONS...
UNKNOWN
SHEDDING NEW LIGHT ON TRUE UNSOLVED MURDER
MYSTERIES LOST IN TIME BUT NEVER FORGOTTEN
JACK SMITH

Printed in Great Britain
by Amazon